Josh and th

Rigby
A Harcourt Achieve Imprint

Greenwood Elementary

www.Rigby.com
1-800-531-5015

Here comes Josh.

Look at the kite.

The kite is going up.

Look at the kite.

The kite is going down.

The kite is down.

Here come the big boys.

Here come Josh
and the big boys.

The kite is going up.

The kite is going

up and up.

The kite is going

up and up and up!